Gentlewomen

Megan Kaminski

NOEMI PRESS

ISBN: 978-1-934819-91-3

Book Cover & Interior Design: Lauren Tobaben

Published By Noemi Press, Inc. a nonprofit literary organization.
www.noemipress.org

Gentlewomen

Megan Kaminski

Contents

NATURA   9

DEAR SISTER   33

PROVIDENCE   41

DEAR SISTER   53

FORTUNA   61

APPENDICES   71

ACKNOWLEDGEMENTS   78

the gentlewomen

NATURA   PROVIDENTIA   FORTUNA

Natura

All seas and water are in my embraces, and the bosom of the earth and the green fields.

THE EXETER BOOK OF RIDDLES

◆

And when day arrived I found most cars
bobbing white amongst waves   paint buffed soft
I washed my mouth with sweetness   tongue
soap-salted so dry it formed film
drawing in the wake against shore
abandoned to rocks to gray
I listened to voices searching for keys
iPhones and so many of my children
floating in the bay catching not on branches
but sky not remembering me not looking
back and still I rolled eastward
bent breath over trees cleared to stumps
carried on through starling swarm
above tall men striding uphill
my voice whispered evergreen shrub
gasped crisp leaf onto roof-tops
sugared pick-ups riding horizons lake-ward
towards crusted reeds, ducks oily-coated feathering
three-o'clock golden wash unto my arms
my daily toil and tender unacknowledged tending
and I watched expanse of water of far-off bush
blackbird scatter filling bleached winter branch
empty promise of buds in December
sedans pad asphalt pot-holed afternoons
bleed my blue children downed in jackets
in fields in metal-fenced feed lots
                    never knowing daylight
just drifting, pink afterbirth on water on lips

the lost girls

This is how we disappear
walking without hesitation into darkness —
    sacks filled with glass bottle and feather
    boots lifting from gravel
    forward to song and snow drift
stars pave paths through commodity wheat
trestle the cold in cottonwood gambrels
these verdant hills, our new mother
grain elevators hold tight and tidy to
            cloud-begotten fields
a daughter who never returns   never disappoints
leaves behind empty rooms and notebooks
filled with sentences writing books to
barricade doors silent in sleep each night

Lake

Slip this morning into my cold depths. I'll cushion you girls
towards polished rocks, smooth your fettered brows. Dark
fish, whiskered and snorting, ammonia emissions chafing bodies,
tumbling sharp edges dull. Secrets drift quietly, children,
trading frog-spawn, mossy logs timbered upstream
for pillow. Nature isn't always nice but if you come inside
I'll share my wardrobe, water-drenched but silken fine: kelp scarves
wrap necks and wrists, chiffon shroud violet-ribboned, pewter noose
saturated with precious stone. Lick ankle, calf, thigh — I devour with
satin tongue.

Velvet Lady

(hear our cries)

brown plush wraps legs
    ribald sun
        ice mooring riverward

white fisherman knots
    white hair un-
        bound to mottled bark

sunk parcels off banks
    you: leaching
        mineral birthing bones

Oh, Natura,

cruel and indifferent mother. You never answer, never come.

Send us into the world without care without sweet cakes

neither a soft bed to sleep nor kind arms to hold.

The world an oyster to step from, Botticelli babe, sweet nothing.

◆

When I rise up strong at times furious,
I thunder mighty and with havoc,
sweep over grasslands over streets
                              when I shake the forest
I fall the boles, split hills, rupture mineral from dirt
I fuck factories spewing smoke, tumble cities,
light oil wells on frozen tundra, metal pipes aflame

I bear on my back all those who once covered
the plains of the earth, their bodies and souls
together in my waters in my dry sands
All mountains and rivers in my embrace
and the bosom of the rising sea, the burning fields

Too dear to carry closely too vast to contemplate
with attention. And I, a mother without mother,
mother to many more than I can or care to hold:
those I bring into the world, those who devour,
who spend in minutes deposits built over ages
on ages, those who turn their backs, who haunt the
forests, and those I return to peaty depths

Lady, ghost-white
  (hear our cries)

    dark ripples pool round
        the bend the
              sky sharpens teeth your

    body lies in weight
        frozen ground
              beside runoff refract

    branched arms sing shadow
        sing root sing
              herbicide-cut memory

◆

Metal scrap through white
brittle trees purple the distance
worn silver like a bruise my legs
abrade snow an island of white
on white extending a breath of pine
I carry each hour leaking from fist
summon arctic fox diving drift deep
I cry for those lost that loss chimed by
lines of trucks filled with injectable water
by tons of saltwater brine exhumed
by black gold burning chimneyed into
fields churchyards evergreen
thickets layer upon layer of shale
still I stead homeward meander
into borderlands into fading light
carry all I can for fractured limbs
bring colder drift to those freezing

the lost girls

Tufts of fur line sun-warmed wood
plastic buttons worn milky
wool threads frayed
      we sit in the corner cabined against
cold nights and bleak noon sun   we carry no I
no we wrapped in lockets silvered
we shadow the sun we hum sweeter sounds we
bring paw-patter in wooden boxes we hold tight
making home making kin with creatures
in fields edging concrete feed bunks
          remembering
a house that burns at night leaves no scar
nor shadow to darken hallways in sleep nor
hot breath cold fingers on still-dreaming neck

◆

I drive spikes into frozen ground
splitting root-flesh tossed
white-ward knit day-dreams
of southern climes but I am
here duty-bound to the center
where the sun drips injection wells
and leaves tongues bitter-coated
afternoon clanging heavy
if the pine gets fell there'll
be stone grits for dinner
fat-back soaked with greens
but what of knitting and my efforts
for quotidian things truculent clouds
impinge upon these hills
squawk endlessly towards
wet ground sprawling pipelines
and I cling to cold sprouts
pray they can dream us home

Furred Lady
(hear our cries)

Dark lean wood fence brush
　　pink chiffon
　　　　frostbit lips iced toes

white sweeps shoulder shaft
　　echo sound
　　　　drag shadow drag tree

gaze shared west drips glass-
　　licked sun
　　　　weeping four o'clock

the lost girls

On the floor of the wash we sort stones
blue and green and yellow accumulate
under fingers under water   clumps of mallow
cling slope-side bitter milked and fat pistiled
        where rusted-out appliances
sprout columbines into fading light
we fatten belly on nettle and peony bud
await whispers from mothers that never come
        being further far better
than evenings in that house   words are
made by hands made by soil
        gather dirt gather sky
        wrap them in cotton and piece the remains

◆

Crows blot ash trees in twilight
calling factories of far off heat
tonight I am a little world sealed in cold
grave memory reseeding for summer
the harvest thistle commanding rifts in clouds
echoing crevasse of Dakota derricks
flaming across plains   I spend daylight hours
slumbering bear-heavy through seasons
to awaken light, sorrows deep in belly
I call mittened hands call snow-shod boots
cake frozen sod to mouth expunge words to air
my subtler longings scatter along prairie
cuckold long shadows   alone I churn night-songs
gum syllables finger down my own cries

Oh, Natura,

too full of love and nurture (with all five of your breasts)!

Too easily depleted and used — your gown oft torn.

Too distant too near too alive with pus and marrow.

Too easily turned tender turned coin.

◆

Late morning sun on roof
old wood stacked low and
mossy wound in the field
scar-pocked snow belies
oil wrenched from shale
poisoned water flowing downstream
but still I sing whole-hearted
spilling forest into weed-poke
fisher cats scream from trees
unfur into shadows merging
mountain into clouds
I listen motherly my nest
entreating longer stays
   no wind no sound no shelter
naked trees signal visitors
valley-ward away from here

Distant hills (undulate)

Deep on the horizon we hold dumb, receiving bodies
into our body by shovel, by drowning, by airplane crash. Arms, legs,
hands, toes — cold broken lanky whole — we receive you. Little by little
light throws shadows dampening horizonal lines softening belly fur.
Blue-green valleys froth mist. Night falls and cries carry underground,
cycling deep into limestone and shale pawing through histories of
bone histories of flesh breaking.

the lost girls

This afternoon we wept   dangled
feet over the frozen creek   listened to cries
echoed from oil patch camps
what happens to her happens to us
our mouths soiled and hands cracking
we looked for prints in fresh powder
bedded down in thick brush
how quiet the evening
              trees hissing through snow
          remembering
the pencil in the piano the knot that came
undone   these remainders of fathers
who grip too tightly of mothers who stay

◆

Across concrete snow-drenched
fields around slaughterhouse on hills
distant over rooftops   cloven-hooved
I slip sweetly into beds warming sheets
whisper consolation for buds budding
early, enticed to frosty beheadings
I wake valleys etched in carbon watch through
oak-lined windows from porches extending
to lawn to wheat to tallgrass-boned prairie
I trudge knee-deep tree to tree-lined bank
noon-light purpling skin and fresh snow
cover cushioning paw to branch-shadow
oceans of expectant ground beneath
my children here my children in wind
joined in arctic thrall

Wreathed Lady

(hear our cries)

Ruffled neck pinked knee
    snow dimple
        warmed bottom and brow

white: the sky the ground
    powdery ice-
        berg sliding up boot

shadows long past noon
    lisp thigh-ward
        draw frostbite draw fire

the lost girls

Lie down on the ground. Lie
down on the ground like that.
And we will carry tree limbs and
bush scrawl. And we will build a fire
to warm paw and foot. Amongst
irrigation tubes and GPS planters, we'll
gather stones from riverbeds and
high-yield seed to pillow fading bodies.
Please just murmur interludes
and rest your head in furry arms.
Let the logs burn and dinners on table
go uneaten quietly slip into memory
a place that warrants no return.

Oh, Natura,

how you love to hide! Always here though never to be found,

and still I seek you!

To look at the world attentively is already to construct a theory.

In my intent looking, I distort the very thing (you!)

I wish to see most clearly.

Snowmelt (yelping)

Leave my silvery shine in shadows spared rough sun. Crystalline cover thins soft underbelly, not spared not swaddled by dry spears below. Brown grass protects local seedlings, zoysia upstarts. Let me stay just a little longer, white iridescent in blue hours. Not pock-marked, not fodder for gray muck, industrial runoff climbing trousers. Brown wash velvets beneath all-weather tires. Small fauna and ferns, I provide shelter from northern exhalations—spread your backs, keep me a few more hours.

Dear Sister

(letters, sent and not)

◆

Losing things levels us all out —
tossing stones into creeks, photos caught
between pages of a novel, necklaces taken
from mother's bureau. These things catalysts

for what next, perhaps. But do not worry;
your letters wait tucked in my jacket lining,
slumbering until a cooler day carries
them nearer my chest and into focus.

It's spring here. Birds chirp relentlessly
and the pink Japanese magnolias out front
weigh down the air. The baby next door's
fat legs dangle from his stroller and

tomorrow or the next day I will write
another letter and pack in it the hazy sun
and greetings from the cup-strewn
lawn and echoes of aging pick-up trucks.

◆

This morning trucks rumbled on the boulevard.
Green ribbons wrapped round trees turned
in the gentle wind, and the cat hissed at bed sheets.
This is a place you pretend does not exist.

These things I see before me — can touch
with hands or linger on brow,
while paper, stiff under fingers, yields not
quite coherent. There is sugar and beets

and whole-wheat flour in my cupboard,
and I would give them all to you if you asked.
The days between us render things insubstantial,
rotten over miles of ocean and lack of salt.

I send you whispers, cotton-wrapped and
gentle-stitched. Perhaps they can carry
another week, bring gray cover to warm days,
loosen tongues to spill greener words.

◆

Spare moments evade me, too. My memory
drips details and I prefer to watch ants scurry
across my bare feet, continuing routes through
dirt onto tree trunk, carrying crumbles to some

unknown destination. The yard is abuzz today:
traffic hums through late morning and girls
chatter, denim-shorted ponytails aloft. And I
wonder why I tell you all this — if you are even

there to receive these missives. My ankles splotched
and bleeding from bramble behind the garden.
When the wind comes up you inhale it whole.
Sun dapples the fields and burnt-out cars

purple the expanse. The lawn burnt from winter
salt and shadow recedes until further notice. I let
my thoughts carry me back inside to honeyed
biscuits and trinkets draped from my wrist.

◆

This shouldn't be so difficult—your side
of the ocean no colder than mine and
coasts are often rocky and lined with stinking
fish and seaweed. I read your letter again

last night when the colder air rolled over hills.
Each line a new complaint about collapsing cupboards
and sulky cats. The neighbors paint their house, white
boards sopped of gray and each morning

a different man on a ladder smiling down to sidewalk.
The trees are still today and everything is quieter.
Voices do not carry through closed windows and only
rumbles from old cars remind me that I am not alone

here in the brick house far from the road. The tea
warms a bit too much and the tray for letters
on the desk still empty, waiting for you to get out
of bed and compose a reply.

◆

I am sorry that your philosophy fails you
so often buckling rickety limbs and sending
you flailing into damp ground. Let's keep
the trucks recreational and worry about other

things. The plant you left is dying, the house
still a mess from last night's fête, and we don't
think so much here about souls (those dusty remnants).
Why don't you forget about crowns and the universe

and come over this afternoon for drinks? Sunlight
covers the backyard and warms the grass and you
might enjoy a break from your brain. We could
cast shadows across the neighbor's fence

to antagonize the dog or just lounge undertree
and measure the passing day. I promise to treat
you more sweetly and hold you close
to trace echoes and thoughts to conclusion.

Providence

I am all that is, all that was, and all that shall be

INSCRIPTION AT THE SHRINE
OF NEITH-ISIS-MINERVA AT SAIS
AS RECORDED BY PLUTARCH

Instructions (how to hold the world)

To encompass and hold and make home. To allow and pass and all to pass through boundaries. The porous body of we and I and they and so. To contain to let wander to give and give and.

To filter through flesh, through soil, through layers of lung and bedrock. To siphon off downstream off diesel tank off currency flow. To misplace capital.

To change and let change. Tissue yielding to branch. Bone to blossom. Each cavern a hive, a swarming into body into sound into dark thump.

To fortify. To merit want and waiting. To carry one heart in another and another, hidden from the world through multiple exposures. Layered film frame on body on open field on landfill.

To give yourself until there is nothing left. To be broken into so many pieces the only option to piece something new. To open to dust. There is nothing and everything and perhaps no you anymore.

I am bell and ghost

throwing dice quietly watching hand
bleed to sky to crow puff and contract
in the cold we are all alone together
sipping coffee while staring at screens
out window into city streets
storm run-off coursing into drains
skin cells peppering the ground
seeding might be and could happen
other ghosts to populate late night walks
confessions of love and other things dm-ed
hands reaching across quarantine zones
feet shuffling through empty halls

I am shadow and siren

stacking receipts in the sun
patently wishing for neighbors to move
from house and also from this wintering
of birds and treeleaf
                         bells toll on the hill
mark the end of morning and quiet and
all that is still in my brain the day sent packing
trudging through commercial district and over
field spreading statistical analysis of CO_2 and
architectural renderings   the floors creak the
walls shake and relations branch phylogenetic the
shift clock sounds day is here and here and here

I am bird-chirp and scabbed knee

tree budding pink sending shadow
across the lawn   murmur into quiet to
construction rattle along the edge of hills
I am trade-wind and lost hours and nose-
nudge under collar pleading for a little taste
a better scent to tuck in my pocket
to gather in my store for keeping safe
and where the day takes you I will follow
and when the sun settles deep in weeds
I will be commodity grain fields silently calling

I am wind and hot wings

tree sway over the valley sheltering
cows and sun-bleached barn   propane tank
and rocking chairs on west-facing porches
I am dried branch bark flake carpenter ant
scuttle through foundation cracks and paths
through hills and two-story falls and sun-peak
I am long buildings of incubating chickens and
feedlot cattle the road sign the burnt field
the truck winding up gravel

I am fly buzz and oak blight

climbing up into sun and
cushioning falls to earth
withstanding wind whip and bird teeter
I am wall creak and warm fire
log crackle and fly swat
teeth tear and hard swallow
grass brown and ATV tracking hills
provision carry and fence mend
I watch and sustain and am
lady bugs gathering on windows
the plastic chair sliding across the lawn
the mileage sign that directs you home

I am stone and stone

becoming blood and bone dissolved
in soil in river carving plateau
coal scar of hill and valley neither
deep nor high and I am hawk call and sweet
whistle tornado siren sounding answer
wetlands drained for subdivision
and cow grazing hillside and branch
decaying by the river and tick that lives
below that log where we rest on hikes

I am strawberry and water-meter

and cars revving engines rounding corners
skimming pavement blurring streetsign
I am grass popping through sideway crack
and squirrel stiffening in the gutter
remainder of breath and tail sway
I am nearer than you know peeping through
slits in the fence through cotton sheets drying
and I am underfoot causing each stumble
fleeing before fall teetering gently undertoe

I am mid-afternoon at the park n ride

snake recoiling after a bite slinking
shadeward under patio drawing darkness
over body slick grass under belly under tail
I am exhaust entering noses coating
sinuses gray and brown-beige muffling sweeter
scents from trees and baking cakes around corner
and I am courier carry: bill notices orders to appear
in court tax documentation contractual obligations
and I am spilling outward bed-bound and grief-stricken
voices saying yes no please perhaps

I am power-line and brush fire

highway unfurling towards northern plains
unspooled unbroken bereft of pulse
carrying to destined location to paycheck to carnage
to small homes far afield with lit fireplaces
and wrought iron pagodas and I am truck whistle
and wind driving snow horizontal biting faces
chilling fingernails blue the wind under eaves
the roof-howl the iced parking lot underboot
the beer in the ice bucket
the clock ticking into the wall

Dear Sister

(into shadow)

She put her ear to the earth

she put her ear to the earth and listened

she put her ear to the earth and listened to what was below

she listened for she who could not listen she who had stopped
    listening long before

she listened for a heart that echoed into concrete and sod and
    subcutaneous rock and water tables and pipelines and
    permafrost and petrified bone forgotten bodies and microbes
    teeming

she listened for her sister whose heart had been swallowed

she listened for her sister whose eyes had been stolen

she listened for her sister who listened and listened with only the
    vibration of footfall on earth above earth below

and what she heard took form formless a gelatinous query into
    inheritance the weaving of texts to keep out the cold what
    seeps through lawns in broad daylight memory of hands and
    sweat and sheets matted skin molting to make way expansion
    of breath and back and sighing into morning

and what she heard

she listened for the dark parts the voices she kept hidden in
    herself bodied in cold storage but she is because she is and her
    sister

is the call into stone as well

is broken and bare and burning the fields scorching ground
seeding for spring deep rooted into prairie
is meadowlark and sandpiper and white-footed mouse and
bluestem and switchgrass

and into gray daybreak a shuffle of letters and poems and photos
across continent a sister passes into darkness (collective echo:
when the wind
comes up you inhale it whole)
and ocean and snow accumulate on cold and hot ground dirt wet
near the coast bedrock sighing waiting the weight of bodies
exhale of expectations

she pours steaming water over green leaves
she pulls a comb through tangles of hair
she types words tentatively at first and then they spool long and
long across the page
she listens for the tufted titmouse and house finch the downy
woodpecker hammering into the side of her house
she listens for the softening of earth the ground beneath ready to
give
she listens to the buds springing open on nearly bare branches to
the squirrel ménage à trois in a nearby tree

and she passed into the sun's heart and out again without notice
the echoes and voices fogged so thick light filtered blue and
purple throned into knowledge and not
a reverberation that passes through the chest warmth leaked
outward passing filtered blood oceanic pulse yielding to the
sun yielding to the moon

she was not done with darkness
she had more time in the dark and so the dark returned dumping
water washing accumulated silt the constancy of cups
emptied and overflowing queened and not forgetting no
reprints no do-overs present unceasing
she watched the green things rain-soaked from her window made
a sharper green in the absence of light unseen radiations
accompanying spring
she felt the days growing longer even though she could not see
them
she listened still atrophied by what she heard and could not see:
raindrops on the banister, fingers buried into fur, exhale
onto pillow, thunder, pesticide soak, call and response of
mourning birds
she also saw the unseen delay of reply syncopation of calls across
oceans misdirected sentences dirt breaking way in spring
tilling longing for longing more than anything else

and one morning she decided to stop waiting and to follow the
     sounds into the lawn and wet asphalt streets into the wheat
     fields into the page through the dark door that leads to long
     hallways and tunnels in the basement of her heart

at the first door she left clover honey at the second her wool
     sweater and the third her bracelet of hydrangeas and at each
     door an offering a striping bare down to what remains and her
     bare arms and legs her cold arms and legs

and what remains was what remained and she saw her self sistered
     dreaming remaindered into a way to forget or remember
     otherwise and she could not hear her sisters' cries or she heard
     them too insistently too close

in the basement's limestone walls down the staircase spider
     sanctuary fiddle-backed and littered year onto year eight years
     wasting down to a slip of a hand a wilted bouquet

waiting beguiled waiting until she could wait and wait for days
     into months and the waiting became what she became a pulse
     halted a breath wanting surface constriction of lungs and
     shoulder and ribcage wanting to rise to drift

and in that waiting she died and was reborn roused by gifts from
     neighboring rabbits by sustenance of voice and vittle and
     gentle song

but she neither knew that she had died nor knew how to live
     only to awaken and arise and to move towards the surface
     ascending into light into morning and day upon day that
     stretched out before

(coo and morning call reverberation into day without response each
    echo an entry a patterning into mold plaster made less distinct
    with each incantation clay pressed into form fingered into carpet a
    blue ribbon a shiny locket
mew-mews laced into chirps itsy entreaties to come closer to rest one's
    head on another's shoulder to warm slowly sun-soaked on the wood
    floor
furnace thrumming afternoons closer last days of artificial warmth
    and sputter
day unenchanted inviting to surface dry-washing shadow into song
    dissolving dust into dust)

so she rose to the day calling sunlight seeped into crevice cracking
    blinded through panels
she rose the mourning and the sticky feeling in her throat that might
    release but choose not to
she rose to light she rose to darkness she rose to the gentle rain on the
    roof sump pumping churning water into sidewalks into street
she rose and rose again spring petals falling like snow like confetti like
    the globe shaken and shaken until all falls upward afloat
she pressed bare feet into dirt into sand into damp grass rooted shallow
she pressed her hand onto her chest and waited for a response

and with each morning earlier light and each night stretching out into
    something else connecting breath to page to heavy cloud

because dawn was still sacred because this rising had to lead other
    than here other than the space that catches in a chest that never
    fully exhales
because she was born because she made planets of her body hip
    circles and ankle rolls stumbling into atmospheric dust and other
    matter the expanse of sky the sweetness of oceans calling
planetary draw away from this place and insertion back again
    calicoed cries and the tiniest bells inviting home
she circled the house, the block, the prairie dwindling to housing
    development and decay
she circled daylight calling more please calling I can't take you with
    me I bind and unbind those lingering hours in burlap rope I
    deposit the remainder for some quiet retreat
she circled the very thing she meant to leave forcing hands through
    thick water salinized weight of years and traveling a place that
    was always and never a place that remains

she steeped tea in glass cups
she searched for an opening a re-entry an escape
she stayed she rooted into bedrock and dirt and ether
she rooted gold calcite and red carnelian
she shifted toes into second position
she rooted deep into soil and drifted in the wind
she swayed and shook with the incoming tide
she wept and wept until she was done with weeping
she stayed she stayed

Fortuna

*"I took thee, naked and destitute as thou wast,
I cherished thee with my substance... I surrounded
thee with a royal abundance of all those things that
are in my power. Now it is my pleasure to draw
back my hand."*

THE CONSOLATION OF PHILOSOPHY, BOETHIUS

And if I walked gently
entered your house in bare feet
toes pressing tile tender
summer coolness wet stone
and if I brought gifts
whispers of perfumed fruit overripe
collapsible mouths coaxing surrender
soft palabras yeasty breath
ocean spray caressing ankles
decked feet sun-warmed wood
arms wrapped rose and violet
and if silver coins pooled parlorside
clinking sweet songs into gambrels
lining garments silken timbre
gamely calling sparrows and gulls
coastward and sea-splendored

my children follow languid
beneath waves and lapsing fauna
singing songs slipped silken
          mother left us beneath the sea
          cockled and bedecked in finery
sputtering upon sand floors
dark hair knotted covering
eyes and ears pulling deeper off-
coast drawn down drawing cold
gold coin jingle paper-lined pockets
skin-lined scarves scarcely keep

the children remember wheels spinning red and
gold flashes   cement blocks piled to draw sand
island strands zonas turistas and pulsating
water turquoise white-tipped and the day
I lost them off the point orange flags waving
west their dazzling death below below

and the birds sing:

In the sky we float our fancies
catching drafts off flat facades
upward using warmth spread
black wings wide hooking
sky float delicious blue scatter
we pither here near there for
shaded homes in cooler climes
seeding secrets promissory notes
leaf and pail heaven-sent sun-soaked
drenched in colored light
lilac-scented breath

I see the banker's wounds, his
weeping eyes
favors cast off
easy like overcoats
misspent coin wasted mettle
if drowning follows darkness
if steel wool softens want
if the wheel turns and turns
raising dust and dung tossing
flowers asunder denting
his fine hat sullying gloves

the businessman sobs at my feet:
"Dear Fortune, be present and propitious
bring sparkle to oars drifting towards
cooler ports receptive waters
deck arms in satin jacquard
merit me prosper and proceed
beneath the waxing moon
velvet tongues to my longings
brick windows watching body
robed in purples red leathered
hands wait in wet receipt"

this prayer this calling out for favor
holds me anchored to each
entreaty each rendering absent
a mother's hand a sister's gaze
drawn interminable want unseen

and the heir cries out:
"Oh horror Oh longing for a new dinner jacket
Oh lady—each hour I misspent in want
for your favors—Oh I beseech Oh I cry
tarry your caresses lapward
if slender fingers cloaked in silver brocade
if trembling lips breathed coin-filled pockets
Oh ascot sullied gray Oh scuffed patent wingtip
Oh limp member Oh me tsk tsk Oh me"

in absence there is darkness in silence
there is grace with each churn of voice
from beguiled men with bellies rumbling
strategic a new plan each hour entreaties
for this and that a purse that must keep
giving each affliction each sigh
rendered less becoming mined ravaged

and the birds sing:
>   *Circling high above the water*
>   *we wait for fish in violet sky*
>   *remaindered calling echo mother*
>   *buried in feathered chest*
>   *summer slipped deeper water*
>   *plastic-choked and swirling out*
>   *cradle-call refuged on rocks*
>   *nested down to mournful chorus*
>   *crying out below below*

our lost bodies beneath the water
polished skin and satined bones
the children smell jasmine and salt taffy
pink scents permeate bedrooms
      flowered wall-to-wall
not abandoned not remembered waiting
in this damp place drownt down district washed
clean scrubbed read by an impatient other
they longed for kept light sailed safe into harbors
rudderless boat moth-loved sails

and I spread my arms
embracing them in chiffon clouds
blue-timbred sea-washed
down-haired arms mouthing
reply to unearned questions
and if my eyelashes deigned
caress their hands seeding red-rashed
wealth fever-hot decamping
promises want for splendor
and if rosettes bedecked dresses
capstans wrung ship to welcome
shores coconut-lined fair-maidened
sultry bones golden chests
spice-drenched gowns
damp sweat-sweetened

and the trader begs:
"Dear lady, I employ you
carry me across seas
I abandon my compass
lay waste to these charts
your mercantile ship
cargo-stacked and gold-gilt
glimmers white upon

open waters given favor
from southern winds
honeyed breathe stoking sails
moon-lit Claribel awaits
in open portico
on distant shores"

and the fund manager:
"Wanton lady, if I could turn
away. Raised only to be left wretched;
my finery flea-infested my furs ravaged
by vermin and mold. The wheel turns
untoward, glancing my way
in spite. Why not fat dividends?
Why not warm breezes on my face,
cool water on my crops, new hair
on my balding skull, and coins
copious falling from sky? Oh me,
falling bedward in despair. Tender lady,
beguile me, whisk me from blustering storms."

and the broker:
"Gentle lady, favor me with your tenders
cooling fevered brow with cool-coined
cure-all. Draw close strawberried lips
candied breath and coax my troubles away.
My pockets swell, my palms tremble
wistful entreats for gouted legs to carry firm
and fast, currency-swapped and option-hedged."

but my children follow faster
hefting raw silk rusted chain
cloved feet piddle over coral
                we'll comfort wounds singe soft metal

soothe burnt eyes with waxen petal
dowries mortgage notes fat-backed choir
wrist-bound baubles bear-toothed trinkets
seed paths beneath currents coaxing ships
lobster pets gurgle half-notes
carry promises reddened gilt

and if I draped their bodies
minked skins to ward off
approaching cold   timbred glass
with gold   bedazzled somber robes
ruby-splendid emerald-clad
if I waltzed them in bespoke suits
and rich perfumes   quiet quadrilles
amber jasmine Moroccan rose wafting
granite halls   tubs cream-filled
for hungry bodies to lap up
and if I allowed them to comb
my orange-blossomed hair
stranding tendrils mild

say the real estate developers as I flee:
"Tender lady upon the water
drop your anchor come ashore
venture to champagne sands
gold-kissed toes tread sod-sought
silken cloaks to shield frost afar"

my fancy lingers feathered
fingering cards and coin on table edge
wide-brimmed and shadowed
dealing aces multiplying hearts
shuffling silk pushed cuffs
elbows festooned blue-ribboned

pointing across the table
shadows linger on bare walls
wood crate seated curl-locked
sodden with milk and dew
the heavenly drone of slot machines

my children pack parcels into days long-spent
sullying memories stacked on shelf
night floods promises misfed remnants
raven-feather swamp-bound unwholesome
came first then fire then yellow sand threadbare
thorn-sodden my hands my eyes my
far-flung cries mingling with weeds below

and the birds sing:
>*And no final eve spent calling*
>*out to waxen ears turned*
>*beyond crowds queued*
>*our charms crack not*
>*nor our mournful chorus*
>*no spirit left for hearts' obey*
>*and stone-cut walls still guide*
>*our soaring into purpled sky*
>*rotting bones yield no reason*
>*scattered amongst this dry decay*

and I sing at last into the night
of plagues and splendor of
wanting until it yields plenty
of red masks in the boardrooms
of red rivers overflowing banks
of red currency through streets
and I and my sisters,
ever present always listening,

tended until our hands blistered
bent until our bones snapped
gave until lungs extinguished aflame
my heart, too, sings out in fever dream
sweat-soaked and staple-sutured
syncopated clock ebony in chest

Appendices

I. NATURA

When Nature brought thee forth out of thy mother's womb, I took thee, naked and destitute as thou wast, I cherished thee with my substance...

- Fortuna speaking in *The Consolation Of Philosophy*, Boethius

The secrets of Nature are hidden; although she always acts, we do not always discover her effects.

- *Préface sur le traité du vide*, Pascal

II. PROVIDENCE

"To be but one with all that lives, to return, by a radiant self-forgetfulness, to the All of Nature."

- *Hyperion*, Friedrich Hölderlin

FRANCISCI PETRARCHÆ
De Remedus
Vtriusque Fortunæ
Libri duo.
Ejusdem de Contemptu Mundi
Colloquiorum Liber.
cum Indiabus duobus

Sapiens Supra Fortunam.

Roterodami,
Ex Officina Arnoldi Leers.
cIɔ Iɔc xl,ix.

III. FORTUNA

"Wise beyond his Fortune"

see: Francis Bacon's treatment of Nature
see: Machiavelli

Fig. 1: Blindfolded Fortune favoring an ape. From Otto van Veen, *Emblemata Horatiana*, Antwerp, 1612 (cat. 79).

By accident most strange, bountiful Fortune
(now my dear lady)

-Prospero in *The Tempest*, Shakespeare

HIS FORTVNA PARENS ILLIS INIVSTA NOVERCA EST

Whatever fortune has raised to a height,
she has raised only to cast it down.

- *Agamemnon*, Seneca

Acknowledgements

I am grateful to the editors of the following journals, where some of the poems have appeared, often in different forms: *Bear Review, Cordite Poetry Review, Dusie, Ghost Proposal, Ladowich, La Vague, Map Literary, N/A Journal, New Orleans Review, Smoking Glue Gun, South Dakota Review, Spiral Orb, Stedt, Stolen Island, Touch the Donkey, Two Serious Ladies,* and *Weave.* I am also grateful to Belladonna* for publishing an earlier version of the poem "Providence" as a limited-edition chaplet.

I am grateful to Brenda Sieczkowski, Anne Yoder, Matthew Hall, and Lesley Ann Wheeler for their enthusiasm and care in reading and responding to earlier drafts of the manuscript. And to Lee Ann Roripaugh, Dodie Bellamy, Bhanu Kapil, Marthe Reed, Duriel Harris, Lisa Samuels, Naomi Falk, Melissa Buzzeo, Ann Vickery, Megan Burns, Marcella Durand, Krystal Languell, Brenda Iijima, Bonnie Roy, Erica Lewis, Michelle Detorie, Misty Schieberle, Forrest Pierce, Matt Burke, Tim Earley, Jessica Comola, Sueyeun Julliette Lee, and Chani Nicholas, for their brilliant comments and conversations that helped to spark and nurture this book.

Thanks to the Hall Center for the Humanities, the Kimmel Harding Nelson Center for the Arts, and the Tallgrass Artist Residency for their support. Thank you to my colleagues and students at the University of Kansas.

My deepest gratitude to Noemi Press and especially to Carmen Giménez Smith and Sarah Gzemski for their faith in this book. An extra special thank you to Lauren Tobaben for giving my poems such beautiful form.

My deep gratitude and love to my sister Caitlin and to my friends and chosen family, who give me essential support and care to live in the world and who encouraged me to write these poems and see them through to book form—Sarin, Brenda, Anne, Jason, Elspeth, Celka, Eileen, Saida, Alexis, Adam, Jessica, Omaris, Maggie, Annie, Kate, David, Lesley, Karl, Sally, Casey, Crystal, and Karla. And for Benny and Brenda, most dear and beloved companions.

About the Author

Megan Kaminski is a poet and essayist, and the author of two previous books of poetry, *Desiring Map* and *Deep City*.

An Associate Professor of English at the University of Kansas and Co-Director of the KU Global Grasslands CoLABorative, she is also the founder and curator of the Ad Astra Project.